S0-BTA-284

WELCOME TO THE U.S.A.
ARIZONA

Written by Ann Heinrichs   Illustrated by Matt Kania
Content Adviser: Jennifer L. Jenkins, PhD, Associate Professor
and Faculty Fellow, University of Arizona, Tucson, Arizona

South Huntington Pub. Lib.
145 Pidgeon Hill Rd.
Huntington Sta., N.Y. 11746

The Child's World

Published in the United States of America by The Child's World®
PO Box 326 • Chanhassen, MN 55317-0326
800-599-READ • www.childsworld.com

Photo Credits
Cover: Brand X Pictures; frontispiece: Photodisc.

Interior: AP/Wide World Photo: 6 (Jeff Robbins), 10 (Jon Hayt), 29 (The Daily Courier/Jo L. Keener), 30 (Matt York); Arizona Office of Tourism: 13; Corbis: 14 (David Muench), 17 (George H. H. Huey), 18 (Tom Bean), 22 (Joseph Sohm; ChromoSohm Inc.), 25 (Richard A. Cooke), 34 (Gerald French); Library of Congress: 16; The Peanut Patch: 33; Photodisc: 9; Tempe Historical Museum: 26; Wickenburg Chamber of Commerce: 21.

Acknowledgments
The Child's World®: Mary Berendes, Publishing Director

Editorial Directions, Inc.: E. Russell Primm, Editorial Director; Katie Marsico, Associate Editor; Judith Shiffer, Assistant Editor; Matt Messbarger, Editorial Assistant; Susan Hindman, Copy Editor; Melissa McDaniel, Proofreader; Kevin Cunningham, Peter Garnham, Matt Messbarger, Olivia Nellums, Chris Simms, Molly Symmonds, Katherine Trickle, Carl Stephen Wender, Fact Checkers; Tim Griffin/IndexServ, Indexer; Cian Loughlin O'Day, Photo Researcher and Editor

The Design Lab: Kathleen Petelinsek, Design; Julia Goozen, Art Production

Copyright © 2006 by The Child's World®
All rights reserved. No part of this book may be reproduced or utilized in any form or by any means without written permission from the publisher.

Library of Congress Cataloging-in-Publication Data
Heinrichs, Ann.
   Arizona / by Ann Heinrichs ; cartography and illustrations by Matt Kania.
      p. cm. — (Welcome to the U.S.A.)
   Includes index.
   ISBN 1-59296-468-0 (library bound : alk. paper) 1. Arizona—Juvenile literature.
I. Kania, Matt, ill. II. Title.
   F811.3.H454 2006
   979.1—dc22   2005011683

Ann Heinrichs is the author of more than 100 books for children and young adults. She has also enjoyed successful careers as a children's book editor and an advertising copywriter. Ann grew up in Fort Smith, Arkansas, and lives in Chicago, Illinois.

About the Author
Ann Heinrichs

Matt Kania loves maps and, as a kid, dreamed of making them. In school he studied geography and cartography, and today he makes maps for a living. Matt's favorite thing about drawing maps is learning about the places they represent. Many of the maps he has created can be found in books, magazines, videos, Web sites, and public places.

About the
Map Illustrator
Matt Kania

On the cover: **What an amazing view! Don't forget to visit the Grand Canyon.**
On page one: **Yeehaw! Be sure to stop by a rodeo in Tucson.**

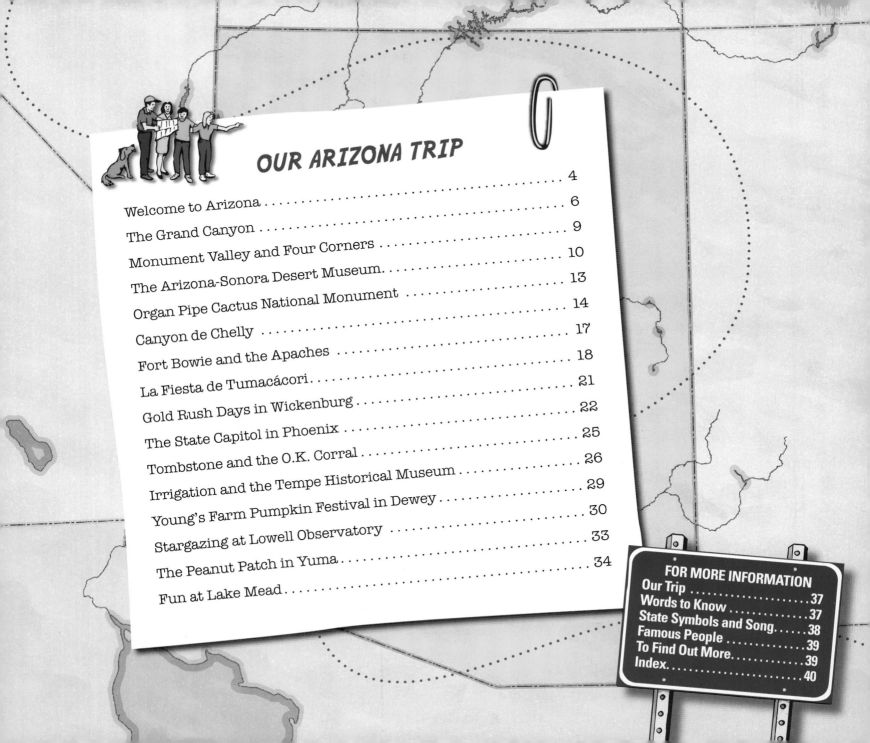

OUR ARIZONA TRIP

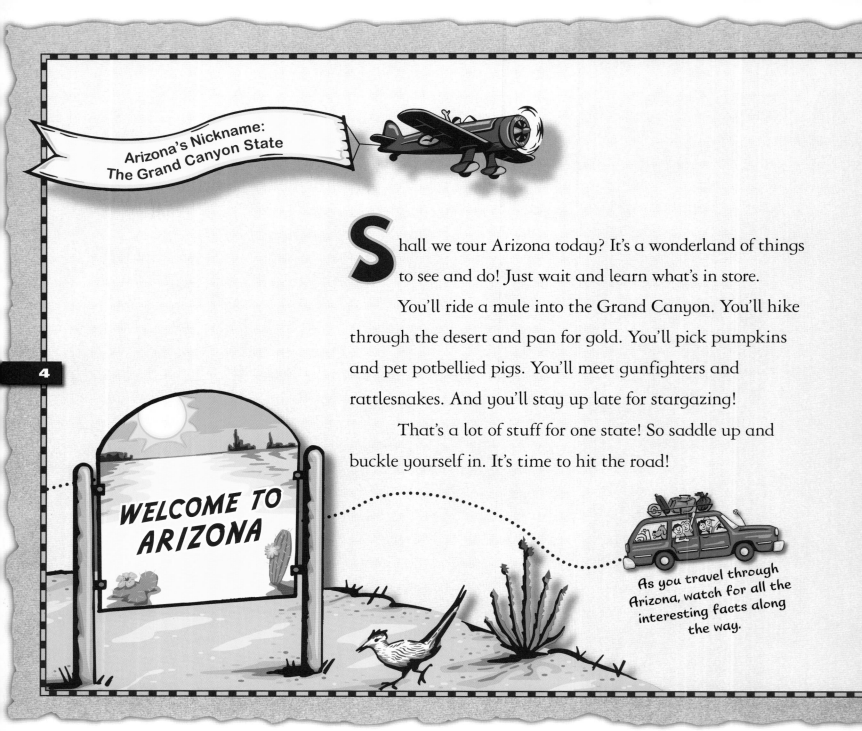

Arizona's Nickname:
The Grand Canyon State

Shall we tour Arizona today? It's a wonderland of things to see and do! Just wait and learn what's in store.

You'll ride a mule into the Grand Canyon. You'll hike through the desert and pan for gold. You'll pick pumpkins and pet potbellied pigs. You'll meet gunfighters and rattlesnakes. And you'll stay up late for stargazing!

That's a lot of stuff for one state! So saddle up and buckle yourself in. It's time to hit the road!

WELCOME TO ARIZONA

As you travel through Arizona, watch for all the interesting facts along the way.

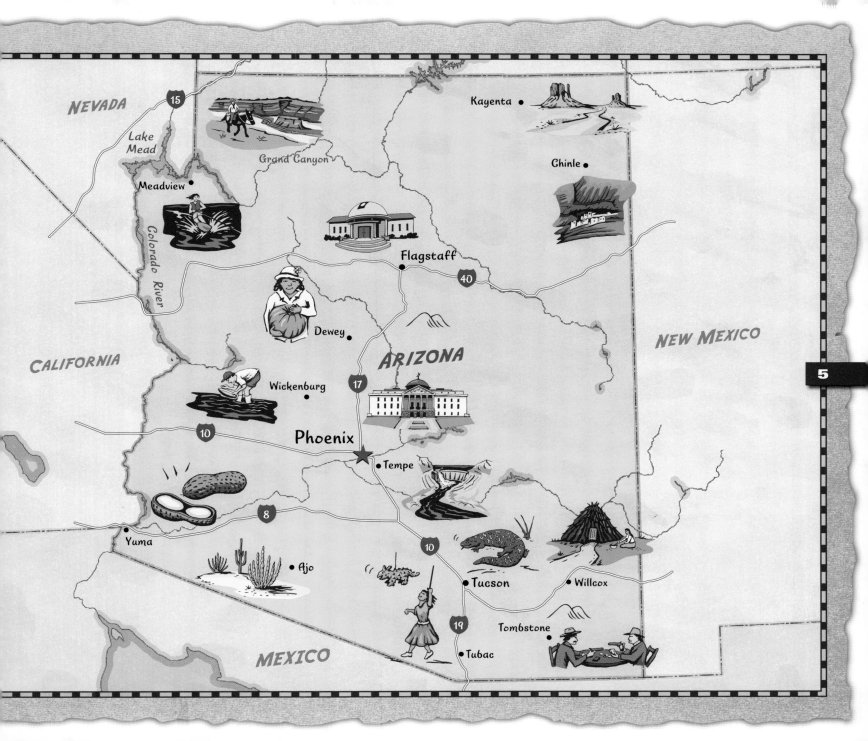

NEVADA

15

Lake
Mead

Meadview •

Colorado River

CALIFORNIA

Grand Canyon

Kayenta •

Chinle •

Flagstaff

40

Dewey •

ARIZONA

NEW MEXICO

5

Wickenburg
•

17

Phoenix

10

Tempe

Yuma •

8

Ajo •

Tucson •

10

Willcox •

19

Tombstone

MEXICO

Tubac •

6

Gila is pronounced "HEE-lah."

Giddyup! Mules carry visitors into the Grand Canyon.

The Gila River runs across central Arizona. The Salt River flows into it. Both these rivers provide **irrigation** water for farms.

Spanish explorer García López de Cárdenas was the 1st European to see the Grand Canyon. He got there in 1540.

The Grand Canyon

Saddle up your mule. Then hop on for a long trail ride. He's taking you down into the Grand Canyon! It's Arizona's most famous natural site. The canyon's colorful rock walls are awesome.

The Colorado River wore away this deep **gorge.** The river cuts across northwestern Arizona. Then it forms most of Arizona's western border.

Highlands cover much of northern Arizona. This region has many mountains and high **plateaus.** Rivers have carved interesting rock formations there. Land in southern Arizona is more low-lying. Deserts cover much of this area. But the south has some mountain ranges, too.

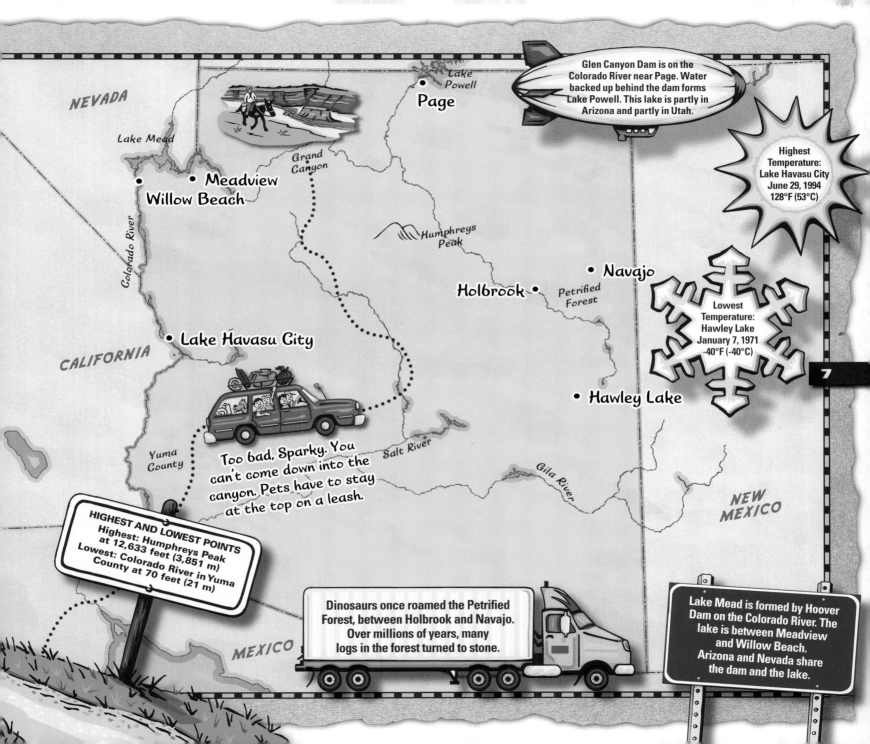

NEVADA

Lake Powell

Page

Glen Canyon Dam is on the Colorado River near Page. Water backed up behind the dam forms Lake Powell. This lake is partly in Arizona and partly in Utah.

Highest Temperature: Lake Havasu City June 29, 1994 128°F (53°C)

Lake Mead

Meadview

Willow Beach

Grand Canyon

Humphreys Peak

Navajo

Holbrook

Petrified Forest

Lowest Temperature: Hawley Lake January 7, 1971 -40°F (-40°C)

Colorado River

CALIFORNIA

Lake Havasu City

Hawley Lake

7

Yuma County

Salt River

Too bad, Sparky. You can't come down into the canyon. Pets have to stay at the top on a leash.

Gila River

NEW MEXICO

HIGHEST AND LOWEST POINTS
Highest: Humphreys Peak at 12,633 feet (3,851 m)
Lowest: Colorado River in Yuma County at 70 feet (21 m)

MEXICO

Dinosaurs once roamed the Petrified Forest, between Holbrook and Navajo. Over millions of years, many logs in the forest turned to stone.

Lake Mead is formed by Hoover Dam on the Colorado River. The lake is between Meadview and Willow Beach. Arizona and Nevada share the dam and the lake.

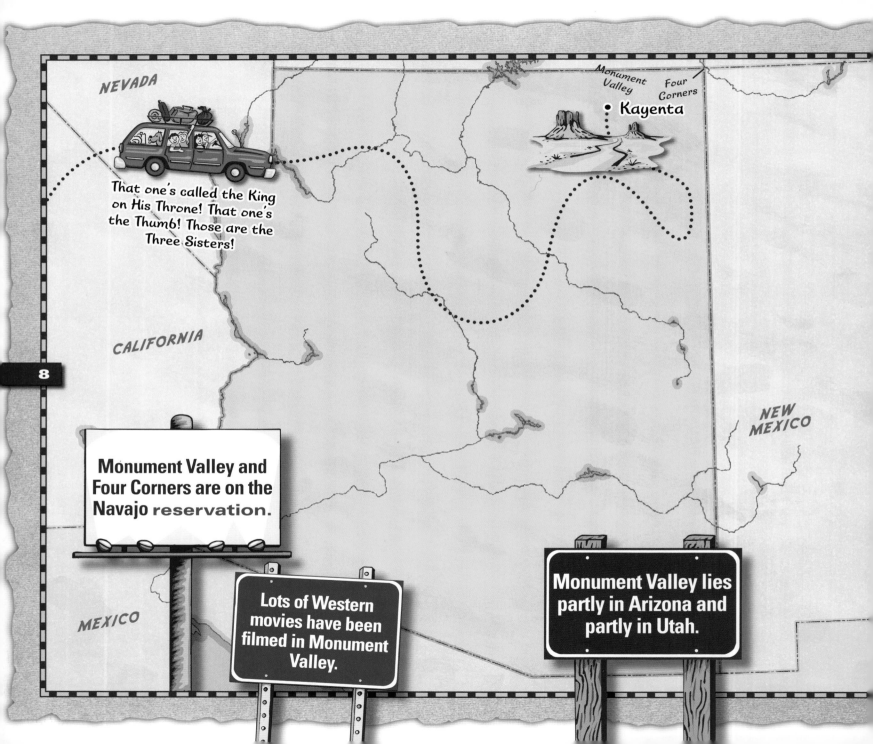

Monument Valley and Four Corners

Have you ever seen a butte? (*Butte* rhymes with *cute*!) It's a rocky hill with steep sides. Just visit Monument Valley, north of Kayenta. You'll see buttes galore!

Two famous buttes are named the Mitten Buttes. They look like a pair of mittens! Another pair is called the Bear and Rabbit. Other buttes are named Elephant Butte and Gray Whiskers.

Next, travel east to the Four Corners. You'll want to stand in this famous spot. The borders of four states come together there. Which states? Arizona, Colorado, New Mexico, and Utah. You can touch all four at the same time!

Want to check out some interesting shapes? Don't forget to visit Monument Valley!

Arizona is home to Kit foxes. They live in underground burrows. They come out mainly at night to hunt.

The Arizona-Sonora Desert Museum

This coati family calls the Arizona-Sonora Desert Museum home. Coatis are related to raccoons.

Wander along the winding trail. Suddenly, you're face-to-face with a mountain lion!

Don't freak out. There's a glass wall between you. You're visiting the Arizona-Sonora Desert Museum! It's in the Sonoran Desert near Tucson. There you'll meet desert animals in their natural surroundings.

You'll see how a rattlesnake's tail works. Prairie dogs will peek out from their burrows. And hummingbirds might even whiz by you.

All these animals live in the Sonoran Desert. So do geckos, horned lizards, and iguanas. But watch out for Gila monsters. They're large lizards with a poisonous bite!

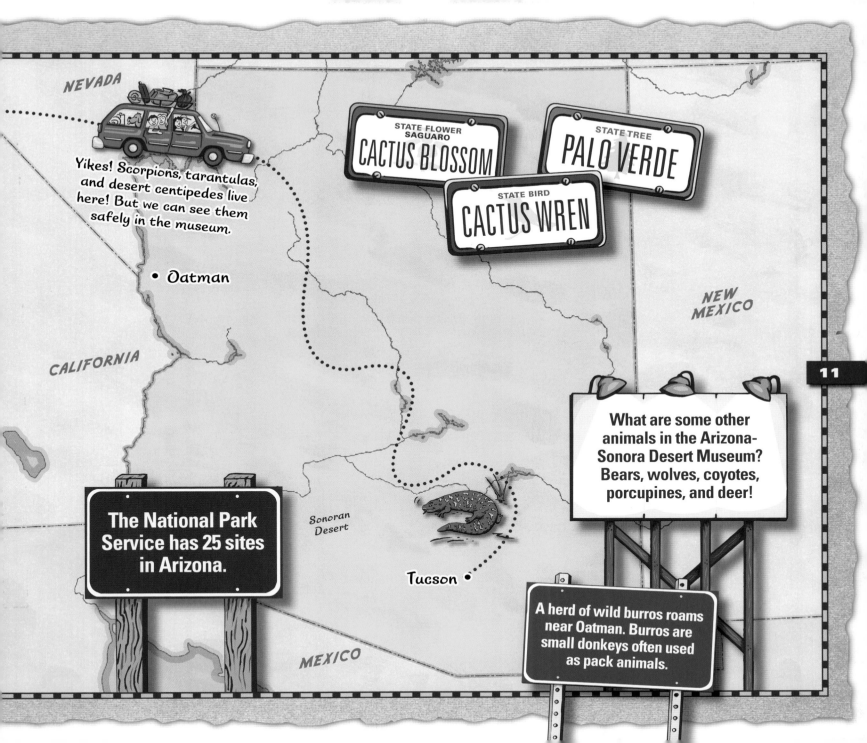

NEVADA

Yikes! Scorpions, tarantulas, and desert centipedes live here! But we can see them safely in the museum.

• Oatman

CALIFORNIA

STATE FLOWER
SAGUARO
CACTUS BLOSSOM

STATE BIRD
CACTUS WREN

STATE TREE
PALO VERDE

NEW MEXICO

What are some other animals in the Arizona-Sonora Desert Museum? Bears, wolves, coyotes, porcupines, and deer!

The National Park Service has 25 sites in Arizona.

Sonoran Desert

Tucson •

A herd of wild burros roams near Oatman. Burros are small donkeys often used as pack animals.

MEXICO

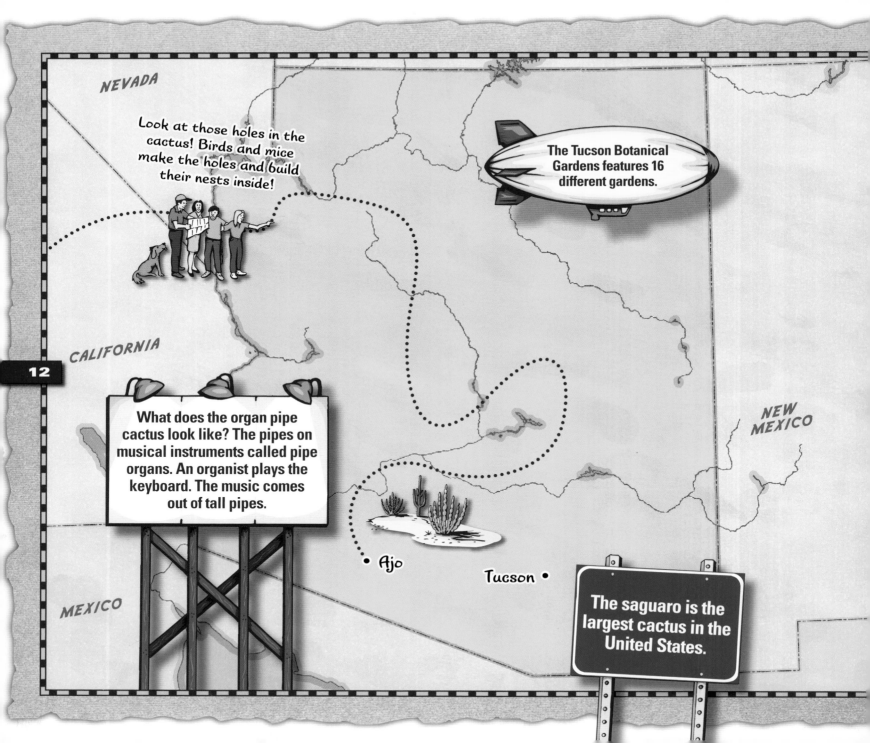

Organ Pipe Cactus National Monument

How many types of cactus are there? Just visit Organ Pipe Cactus National Monument. It's south of Ajo on the Mexican border. You'll see twenty-six types of cactus there!

All kinds of cactus grow in Arizona. Some are saguaro (sah-WAH-ro), cholla (CHO-yah), beavertail, and hedgehog cactus. Each one has a special shape and size. It's easy to spot the organ pipe cactus. Its tall arms branch out from the base.

Saguaro National Park is near Tucson. Giant saguaro cactus grow there. Some are as tall as five-story buildings. They look like people holding their arms up!

Take a peek at this organ pipe cactus! Does it remind you of a musical instrument?

Nopalitos are the tender pads of the prickly pear cactus. In **Hispanic** culture, they're a delicious food!

Canyon de Chelly

Don't miss Canyon de Chelly near Chinle. (*Chelly* is pronounced "SHAY.") You'll see homes high in the canyon walls. It's hard to imagine how they were built! They're ancient dwellings of the Anasazi people. They lived here more than 1,000 years ago.

The Hohokam lived in central Arizona. They built a massive irrigation system. It brought water to their crops. The Mogollon lived in eastern Arizona.

Spanish explorers arrived in the 1500s. They were looking for **legendary** cities of gold. **Missionaries** came to spread Christianity, too. Spain ruled this region until 1821. Then it became part of Mexico. It passed to the United States in 1848.

There's no place like home! Anasazi people used to live in Canyon de Chelly.

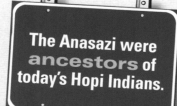

The Anasazi were **ancestors** of today's Hopi Indians.

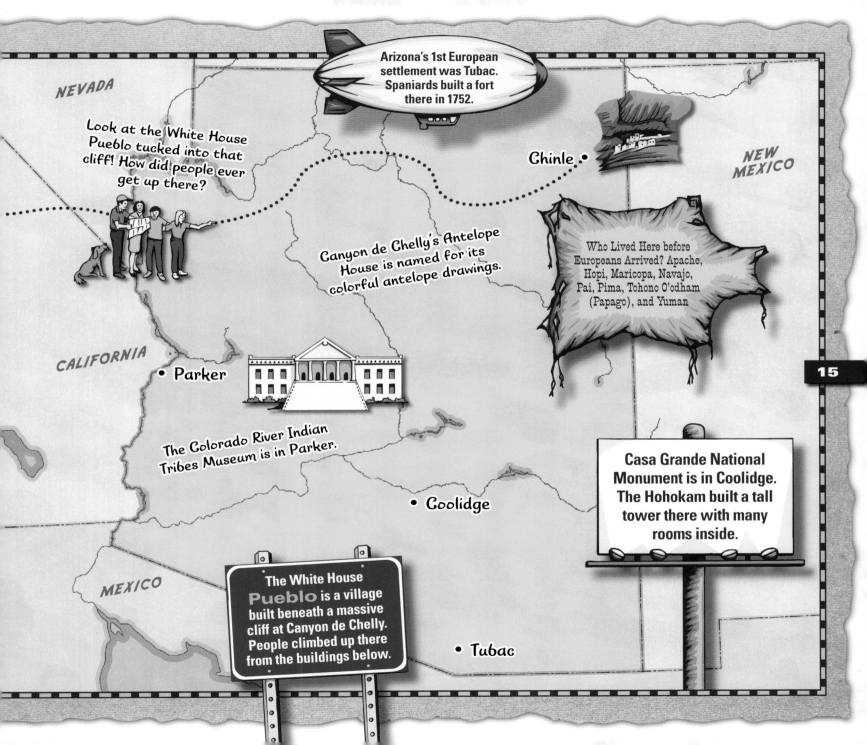

NEVADA

Arizona's 1st European settlement was Tubac. Spaniards built a fort there in 1752.

Look at the White House Pueblo tucked into that cliff! How did people ever get up there?

Chinle •

NEW MEXICO

Canyon de Chelly's Antelope House is named for its colorful antelope drawings.

Who Lived Here before Europeans Arrived? Apache, Hopi, Maricopa, Navajo, Pai, Pima, Tohono O'odham (Papago), and Yuman

CALIFORNIA

• Parker

15

The Colorado River Indian Tribes Museum is in Parker.

Casa Grande National Monument is in Coolidge. The Hohokam built a tall tower there with many rooms inside.

• Coolidge

MEXICO

The White House Pueblo is a village built beneath a massive cliff at Canyon de Chelly. People climbed up there from the buildings below.

• Tubac

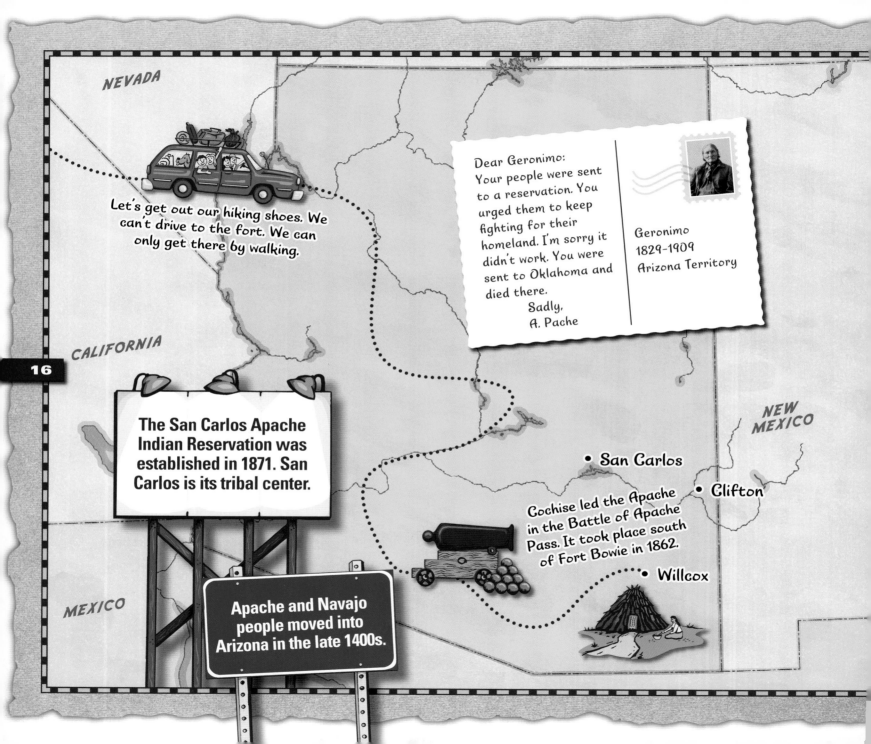

Let's get out our hiking shoes. We can't drive to the fort. We can only get there by walking.

Dear Geronimo:
Your people were sent to a reservation. You urged them to keep fighting for their homeland. I'm sorry it didn't work. You were sent to Oklahoma and died there.
          Sadly,
          A. Pache

Geronimo
1829-1909
Arizona Territory

The San Carlos Apache Indian Reservation was established in 1871. San Carlos is its tribal center.

Apache and Navajo people moved into Arizona in the late 1400s.

• San Carlos

• Clifton

Cochise led the Apache in the Battle of Apache Pass. It took place south of Fort Bowie in 1862.

• Willcox

NEVADA

CALIFORNIA

MEXICO

NEW MEXICO

Hike the trail to Fort Bowie, near Willcox. You'll pass an old stagecoach station. Then you'll pass an Apache wickiup, or hut. Finally, you reach the fort. There you'll see where soldiers ate and slept.

Many settlers moved into Arizona in the mid-1800s. The Apache Indians tried to keep their land. They attacked ranches, forts, and towns. Fort Bowie's army troops fought them.

Cochise and Geronimo were Apache leaders. They just kept on fighting. Cochise was forced to give up in 1872. The army promised Geronimo safety for his followers. So Geronimo gave up in 1886. Then he and his people were jailed.

Travel back to the 1800s! Tour historic ruins at Fort Bowie.

17

Geronimo was born in what later became known as Clifton.

18

La Fiesta de Tumacácori

See a puppet show and swat a **piñata.** Watch Native American dancers and dashing horsemen. Taste loads of spicy, mouthwatering foods. You're at La Fiesta de Tumacácori! It celebrates Indian, Hispanic, and **Anglo** customs. These are Arizona's three major **cultures.**

Many Arizona cities have Hispanic or Indian names. Casa Grande, Tucson, and Yuma are examples. Hispanic and Indian foods are popular in Arizona, too. Arizonans enjoy a great mix of cultures!

Thousands of people move to Arizona every year. They love the sunny climate. Arizona has grown since 1950. Almost seven times more people live there now!

Feel like dancing? These performers are part of La Fiesta de Tumacácori.

About 1 out of 20 Arizonans is Indian. Only California and Oklahoma have more Native Americans than Arizona.

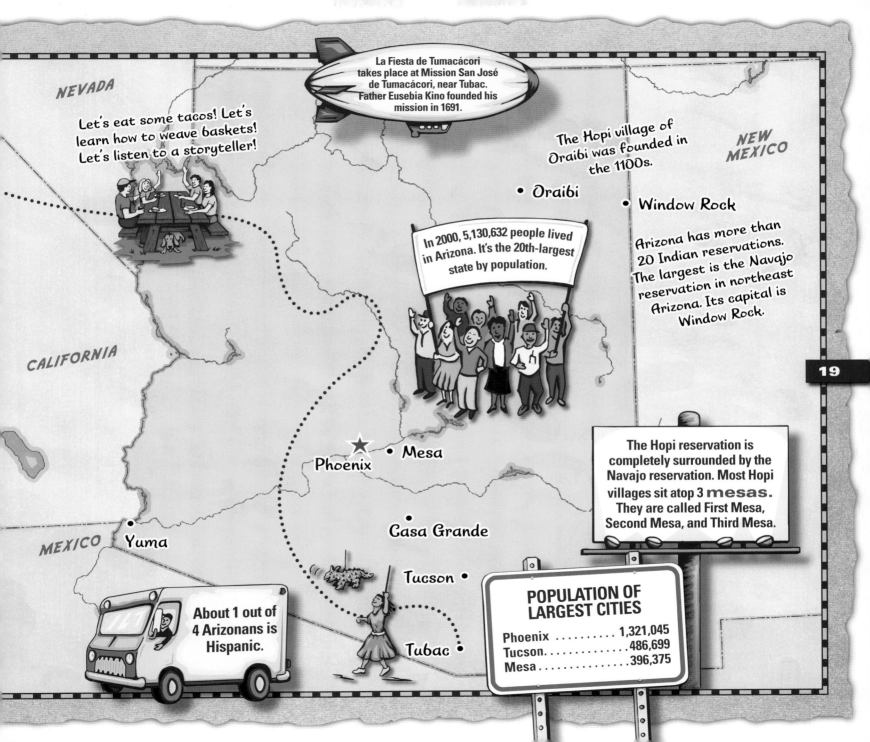

La Fiesta de Tumacácori takes place at Mission San José de Tumacácori, near Tubac. Father Eusebia Kino founded his mission in 1691.

Let's eat some tacos! Let's learn how to weave baskets! Let's listen to a storyteller!

NEVADA

NEW MEXICO

The Hopi village of Oraibi was founded in the 1100s.

• Oraibi

• Window Rock

Arizona has more than 20 Indian reservations. The largest is the Navajo reservation in northeast Arizona. Its capital is Window Rock.

In 2000, 5,130,632 people lived in Arizona. It's the 20th-largest state by population.

CALIFORNIA

19

The Hopi reservation is completely surrounded by the Navajo reservation. Most Hopi villages sit atop 3 **mesas**. They are called First Mesa, Second Mesa, and Third Mesa.

★ Phoenix   • Mesa

MEXICO   • Yuma

• Casa Grande

About 1 out of 4 Arizonans is Hispanic.

Tucson •

Tubac •

POPULATION OF LARGEST CITIES

Phoenix 1,321,045
Tucson 486,699
Mesa 396,375

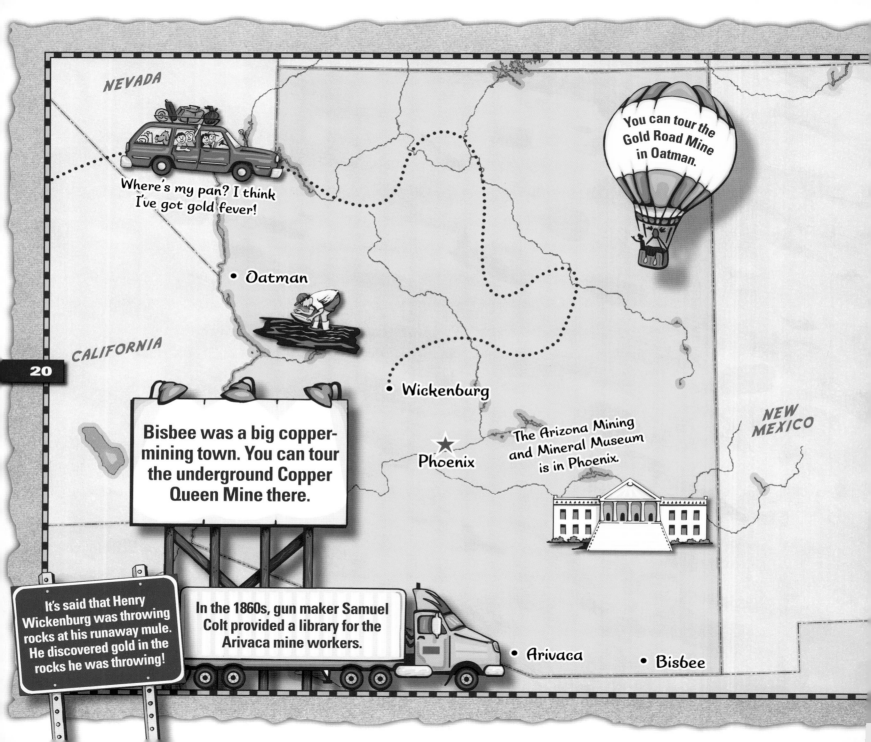

NEVADA

Where's my pan? I think I've got gold fever!

You can tour the Gold Road Mine in Oatman.

• Oatman

CALIFORNIA

• Wickenburg

Bisbee was a big copper-mining town. You can tour the underground Copper Queen Mine there.

★ Phoenix

The Arizona Mining and Mineral Museum is in Phoenix.

NEW MEXICO

It's said that Henry Wickenburg was throwing rocks at his runaway mule. He discovered gold in the rocks he was throwing!

In the 1860s, gun maker Samuel Colt provided a library for the Arivaca mine workers.

• Arivaca

• Bisbee

Gold Rush Days in Wickenburg

Are you good at mucking? That means shoveling **ore** into a cart. Maybe you're good at panning for gold. You hold a pan in a running stream. If you're lucky, your pan might catch grains of gold!

You can enter contests for all these activities. Just drop by Wickenburg for Gold Rush Days! This festival celebrates an exciting time in history. Henry Wickenburg discovered gold in the area in 1863. Thousands of people swarmed in to get rich!

Both gold and silver were found in Arizona. But copper had long-lasting success. Copper-mining towns sprang up around Arizona. Now it's the top copper-mining state!

Would you have been good at mucking? Find out at Gold Rush Days in Wickenburg!

What's Mined in Arizona? Copper and sand and gravel

Lawmakers are hard at work inside Arizona's capitol.

Stewart Udall was born in Saint Johns. He was U.S. secretary of the interior from 1961 to 1969.

The State Capitol in Phoenix

Arizona mines lots of copper. Where does that copper go? All over the world. But some of it stays right at home. Just look at the state capitol. Its roof and dome are covered with copper!

This building is the center of state government. Arizona's government is organized like the U.S. government. It has three branches. One branch makes the state's laws. Another branch enforces the laws. That means making sure the laws are obeyed. The governor heads this branch. Judges make up the third branch. They listen to cases in court. Then they decide whether someone has broken a law.

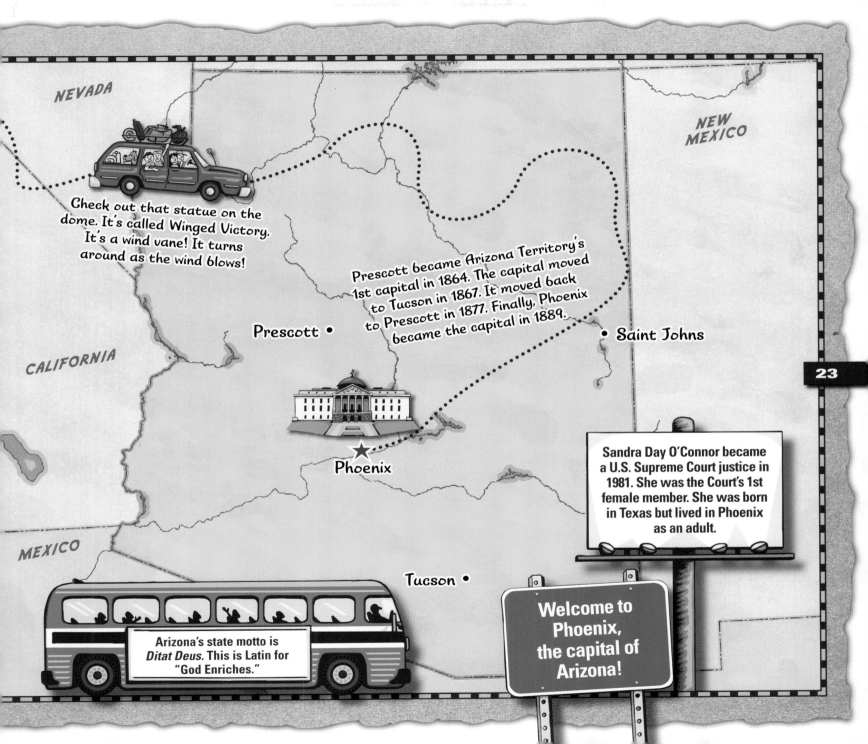

NEVADA

NEW MEXICO

Check out that statue on the dome. It's called Winged Victory. It's a wind vane! It turns around as the wind blows!

Prescott became Arizona Territory's 1st capital in 1864. The capital moved to Tucson in 1867. It moved back to Prescott in 1877. Finally, Phoenix became the capital in 1889.

CALIFORNIA

Prescott •

• Saint Johns

★
Phoenix

Sandra Day O'Connor became a U.S. Supreme Court justice in 1981. She was the Court's 1st female member. She was born in Texas but lived in Phoenix as an adult.

MEXICO

Tucson •

Arizona's state motto is *Ditat Deus*. This is Latin for "God Enriches."

Welcome to Phoenix, the capital of Arizona!

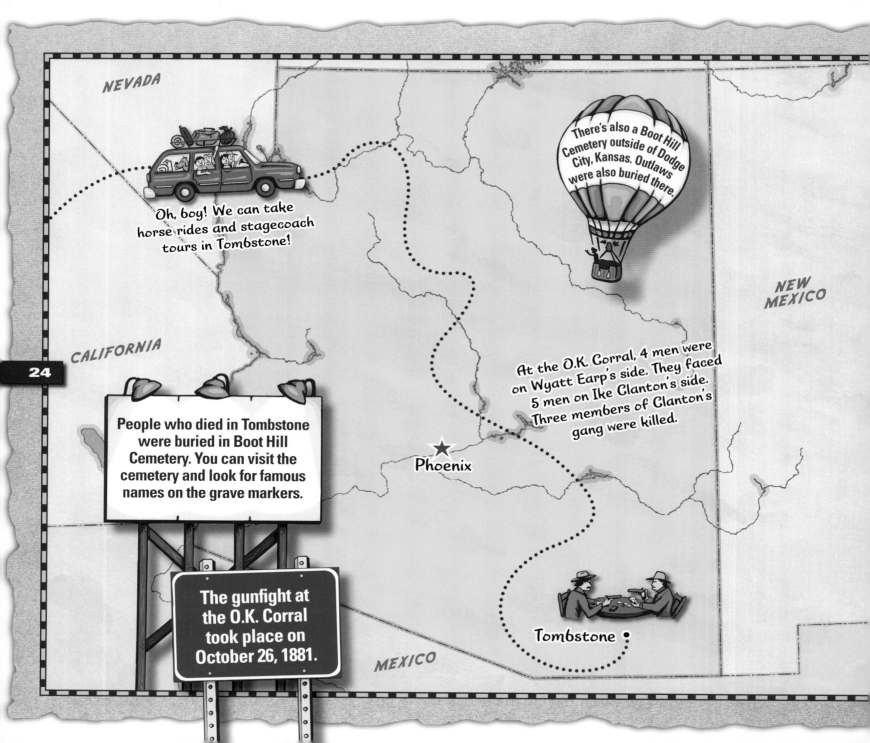

NEVADA

NEW MEXICO

CALIFORNIA

There's also a Boot Hill Cemetery outside of Dodge City, Kansas. Outlaws were also buried there.

Oh, boy! We can take horse rides and stagecoach tours in Tombstone!

At the O.K. Corral, 4 men were on Wyatt Earp's side. They faced 5 men on Ike Clanton's side. Three members of Clanton's gang were killed.

People who died in Tombstone were buried in Boot Hill Cemetery. You can visit the cemetery and look for famous names on the grave markers.

★ Phoenix

The gunfight at the O.K. Corral took place on October 26, 1881.

MEXICO

Tombstone •

Tombstone and the O.K. Corral

The gunfighters look pretty mean. Suddenly, they draw their guns. Bang, bang! In a few puffs of smoke, it's over.

Don't worry. No one really gets shot. You're watching a show in Tombstone. People are acting out a famous scene. It's the gunfight at the O.K. Corral!

Tombstone was once a pretty wild town. Silver was discovered there in 1877. Thousands of people rushed in. They sometimes settled their quarrels with guns. That's what happened at the O.K. Corral.

Nine men took part in the historic gunfight. The most famous gunman was Wyatt Earp. He's the subject of many movies and TV shows!

Pow! Should you run for cover? No, Tombstone treats visitors to gunfight shows.

Pioneer Arizona Living History Village is near Phoenix. It's built like a town from Arizona Territory days.

Want to see a model of the Salt River? Just head to the Tempe Historical Museum.

Hoover Dam was completed in 1936. It straddles the Arizona–Nevada border near Willow Beach.

Irrigation and the Tempe Historical Museum

Would you like to create an irrigation system? Just visit the Tempe Historical Museum. It has a huge model of the Salt River. You can direct its waters into **canals** and fields!

Arizona has big irrigation systems. They were created by building dams on rivers. Water builds up behind the dams. Then it's sent through irrigation canals. The dams create electricity with water power, too.

Arizona built several dams on the Salt River. One was Roosevelt Dam, near Roosevelt. It opened in 1911. The Gila River's Coolidge Dam opened in 1928. It's near San Carlos. The Colorado River was dammed, too.

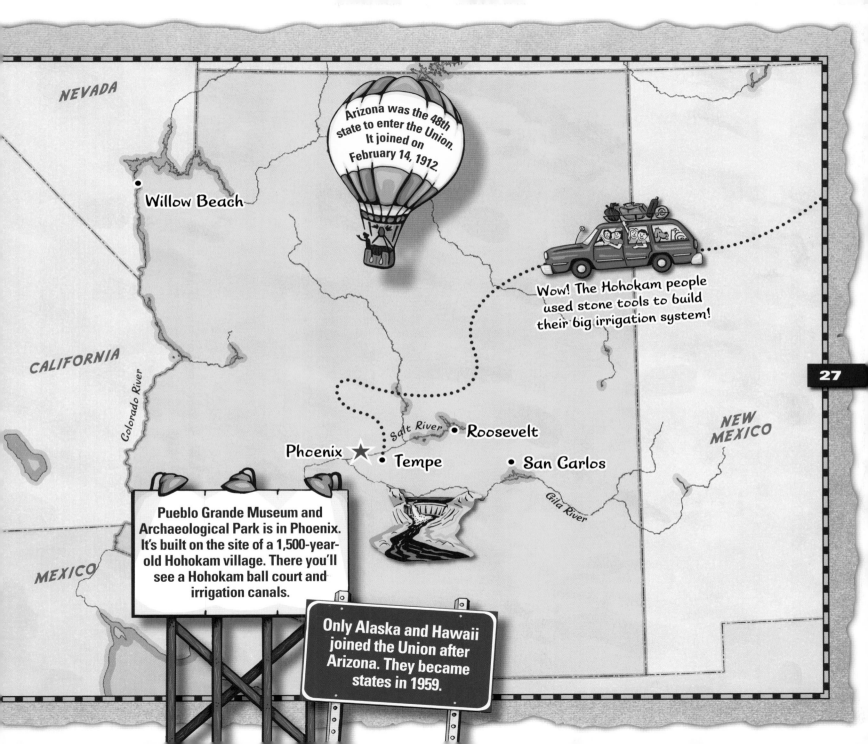

NEVADA

Willow Beach

Arizona was the 48th state to enter the Union. It joined on February 14, 1912.

Wow! The Hohokam people used stone tools to build their big irrigation system!

CALIFORNIA

Colorado River

27

NEW MEXICO

Salt River

Phoenix ★ ● Tempe

● Roosevelt

● San Carlos

Gila River

Pueblo Grande Museum and Archaeological Park is in Phoenix. It's built on the site of a 1,500-year-old Hohokam village. There you'll see a Hohokam ball court and irrigation canals.

MEXICO

Only Alaska and Hawaii joined the Union after Arizona. They became states in 1959.

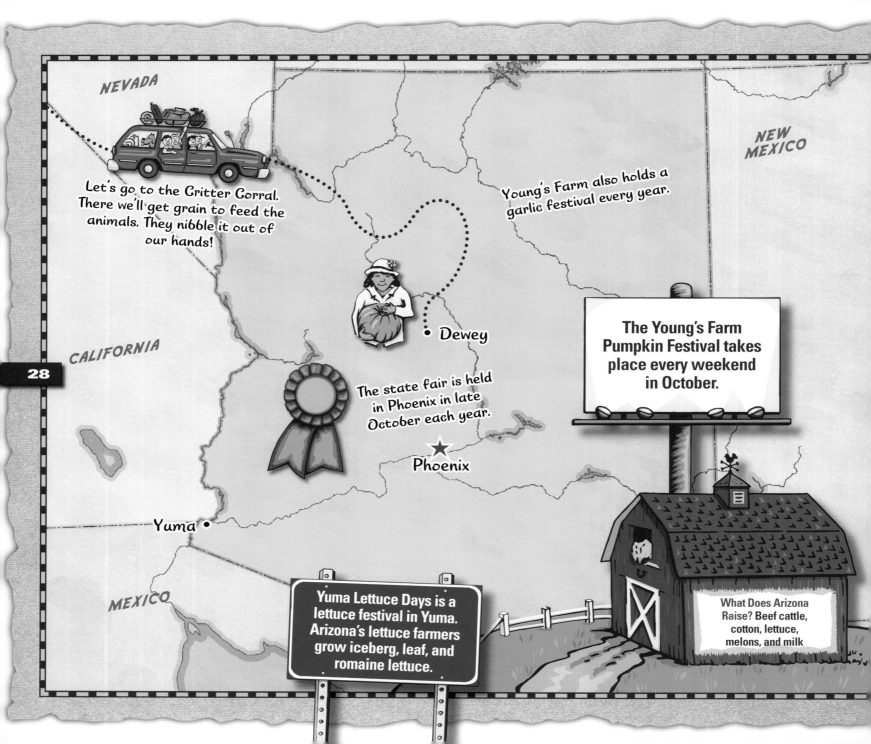

NEVADA

NEW MEXICO

Let's go to the Critter Corral. There we'll get grain to feed the animals. They nibble it out of our hands!

Young's Farm also holds a garlic festival every year.

CALIFORNIA

• Dewey

The Young's Farm Pumpkin Festival takes place every weekend in October.

The state fair is held in Phoenix in late October each year.

★
Phoenix

Yuma •

MEXICO

Yuma Lettuce Days is a lettuce festival in Yuma. Arizona's lettuce farmers grow iceberg, leaf, and romaine lettuce.

What Does Arizona Raise? Beef cattle, cotton, lettuce, melons, and milk

Farms throughout much of Arizona receive irrigation water.

Ride a hay wagon to the pumpkin patch. Then pick your own Halloween pumpkin. Be sure to visit the Critter Corral. You'll see goats, sheep, and potbellied pigs. You're enjoying the Young's Farm Pumpkin Festival!

Arizonans are proud of their many farm products. The state's leading crop is lettuce. Cotton is important, too. Many farmers grow citrus fruits. That includes lemons, oranges, and grapefruits.

Beef cattle graze on big ranches in Arizona. You'll see sheep nibbling the grasses, too. Is it springtime? Then you'll see new lambs prancing around!

29

Yikes! Bad luck! A black cat prowls through Dewey's pumpkin patch.

Feel like exploring another planet? Visitors tour the Pluto Dome at Lowell Observatory.

About 30 large telescopes are positioned on the mountains around Tucson.

Stargazing at Lowell Observatory

What does the Moon's surface look like? How about Saturn, Jupiter, and Mars? You'll see them all at Lowell Observatory in Flagstaff! Just take a nighttime tour. You can gaze through its massive telescope.

Arizona's clear skies come in handy. Scientists can see objects in space clearly. An astronomer at Lowell Observatory found that out. He discovered the planet Pluto in 1930.

Clear skies are good for airplane pilots, too. This was helpful during World War II (1939–1945). Many military air bases opened in Arizona. After the war, Arizona's population soared. Thousands of people decided to settle there.

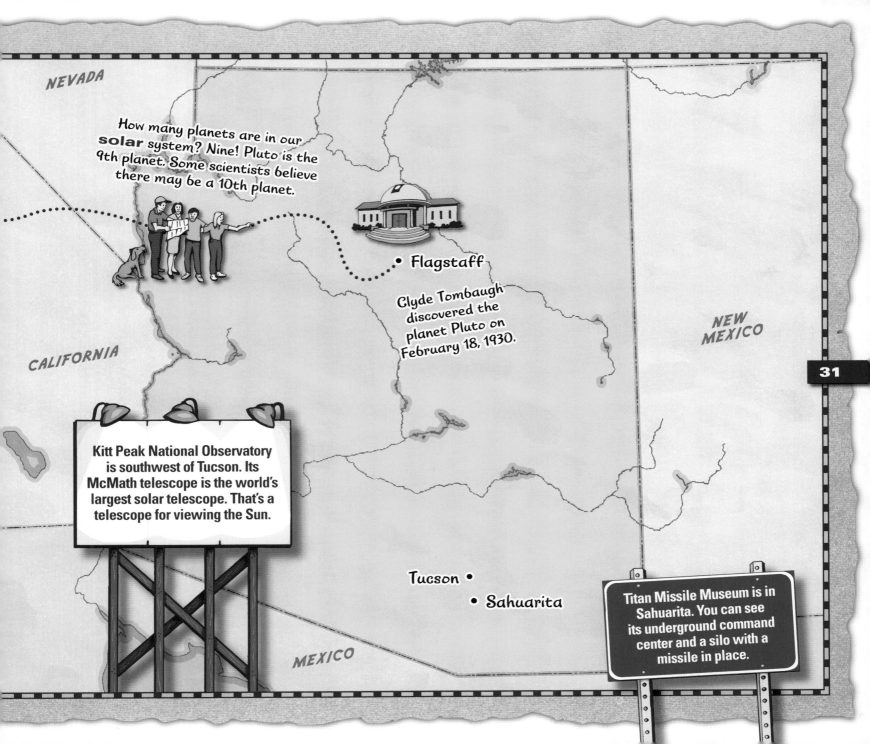

NEVADA

How many planets are in our **solar** system? Nine! Pluto is the 9th planet. Some scientists believe there may be a 10th planet.

• Flagstaff

Clyde Tombaugh discovered the planet Pluto on February 18, 1930.

CALIFORNIA

NEW MEXICO

Kitt Peak National Observatory is southwest of Tucson. Its McMath telescope is the world's largest solar telescope. That's a telescope for viewing the Sun.

Tucson •

• Sahuarita

Titan Missile Museum is in Sahuarita. You can see its underground command center and a silo with a missile in place.

MEXICO

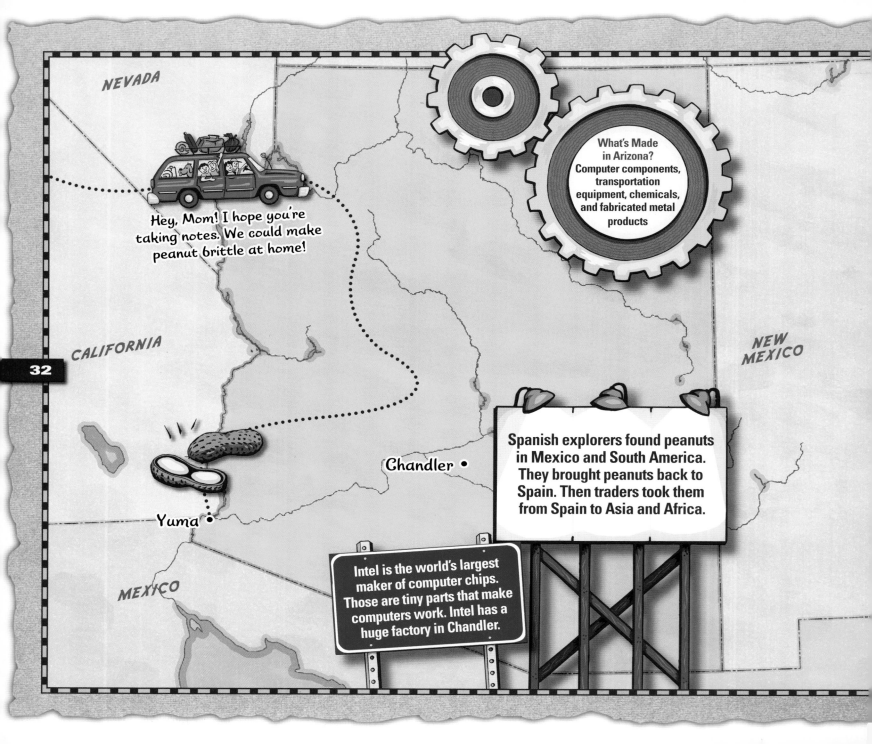

The Peanut Patch in Yuma

Are you hungry? Make a pit stop at Yuma's Peanut Patch!

Watch workers dump the peanuts into roasters. Then chomp on a warm, freshly roasted peanut. Next, watch machines grind the peanuts up. They might end up as peanut butter. Some peanuts go to the candy kitchen. They're made into peanut brittle and peanut fudge!

You're touring the Peanut Patch. This food factory makes delicious things with peanuts.

Arizona makes many food products. But computer equipment is the top factory item. Some factories make radios and TVs. Others make aircraft, spacecraft, missiles, or metals.

Hop aboard a float! It's time for the Fiesta Bowl parade!

Fun at Lake Mead

You could spend weeks at Lake Mead! It's in Arizona's northwest corner, near Meadview. You can go boating, swimming, or fishing. Then you can explore the surrounding desert. Mountains and canyon walls rise in the distance.

Arizona's a great place for outdoor fun. In the winter, people come from cold states. They enjoy Arizona's warm weather. Meanwhile, skiers flock to the snowy mountains.

The Fiesta Bowl is an exciting sports festival. Fiesta Bowl events happen around New Year's Day. First, there's a big parade in Phoenix. Then college football champs play in Tempe. Thousands of people join in the fun!

Many baseball teams have their spring training in the Phoenix area.

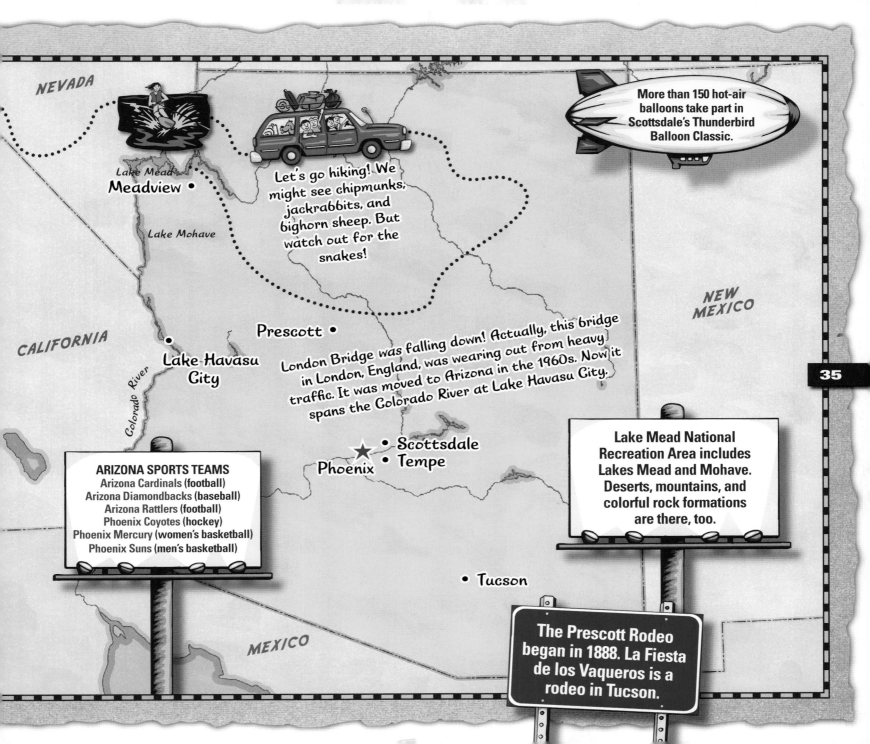

NEVADA

CALIFORNIA

Lake Mead
Meadview •

Lake Mohave

More than 150 hot-air balloons take part in Scottsdale's Thunderbird Balloon Classic.

NEW MEXICO

Let's go hiking! We might see chipmunks, jackrabbits, and bighorn sheep. But watch out for the snakes!

Prescott •

London Bridge was falling down! Actually, this bridge in London, England, was wearing out from heavy traffic. It was moved to Arizona in the 1960s. Now it spans the Colorado River at Lake Havasu City.

Lake Havasu City •

★ • **Scottsdale**
Phoenix • **Tempe**

Lake Mead National Recreation Area includes Lakes Mead and Mohave. Deserts, mountains, and colorful rock formations are there, too.

ARIZONA SPORTS TEAMS
Arizona Cardinals (football)
Arizona Diamondbacks (baseball)
Arizona Rattlers (football)
Phoenix Coyotes (hockey)
Phoenix Mercury (women's basketball)
Phoenix Suns (men's basketball)

• **Tucson**

MEXICO

The Prescott Rodeo began in 1888. La Fiesta de los Vaqueros is a rodeo in Tucson.

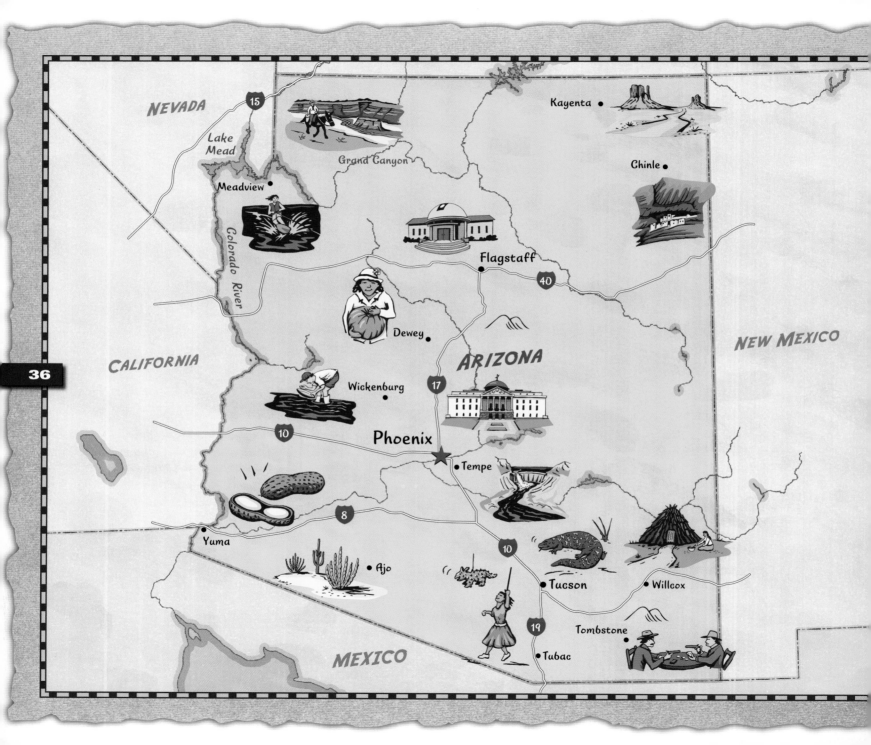

OUR TRIP

We visited many amazing places on our trip! We also met a lot of interesting people along the way. Look at the map on the left. Use your finger to trace all the places we have been.

Who was the 1st European to see the Grand Canyon? See page 6 for the answer.

What type of animal roams near Oatman? Page 11 has the answer.

What is the largest cactus in the United States? See page 12 for the answer.

Where was Geronimo born? Look on page 17 for the answer.

Who was Stewart Udall? Page 22 has the answer.

When was Hoover Dam completed? Turn to page 26 for the answer.

Where is the state fair held every year? Look on page 28 for the answer.

Who discovered Pluto? Turn to page 31 for the answer.

That was a great trip! We have traveled all over Arizona!

There are a few places that we didn't have time for, though. Next time, we plan to visit the Reid Park Zoo in Tucson. This zoo features more than 500 animals, including African elephants and piranhas! Kids can take part in classes and camps that teach about conservation.

More Places to Visit in Arizona

WORDS TO KNOW

ancestors (AN-sess-turz) a person's grandparents, great-grandparents, and so on

Anglo (ANG-low) descended from non-Hispanic European people

canals (kuh-NALZ) long ditches dug to create a waterway for travel or watering crops

cultures (KUHL-churz) various people's beliefs, customs, and ways of life

gorge (GORJ) a deep valley, often cut through rock by a river

Hispanic (hiss-PAN-ik) having roots in Spanish-speaking lands

irrigation (ihr-uh-GAY-shuhn) directing water from rivers or lakes into fields

legendary (LEJ-uhn-dair-ee) based on fantastic stories

mesas (MAY-suhz) steep-sided hills or mountains with flat tops

missionaries (MISH-uh-nair-eez) people who travel somewhere to spread their faith

ore (OR) rock that contains valuable minerals such as silver or gold

piñata (pin-YAH-tah) an animal figure filled with candy

plateaus (plah-TOZ) regions of high, level land

pueblo (PUEH-blow) a village

reservation (reh-zuhr-VAY-shuhn) land set aside for Indians

solar (SO-lur) relating to the Sun

Arizona covers 113,635 square miles (294,312 sq km). It's the 6th-largest state in size.

STATE SYMBOLS

State amphibian: Arizona tree frog

State bird: Cactus wren

State butterfly: Two-tailed swallowtail

State fish: Apache trout

State flower: Saguaro cactus blossom

State fossil: Petrified wood

State gemstone: Turquoise

State mammal: Ringtail

State neckwear: Bola tie

State reptile: Arizona ridge-nosed rattlesnake

State tree: Palo verde

State flag

State seal

STATE SONGS

"Arizona March Song"
*Words by Margaret Rowe Clifford,
music by Maurice Blumenthal*

Come to this land of sunshine
To this land where life is young.
Where the wide, wide world is waiting,
The songs that will now be sung.
Where the golden sun is flaming
Into warm, white shining day,
And the sons of men are blazing
Their priceless right of way.

Come stand beside the rivers
Within our valleys broad.
Stand here with heads uncovered,
In the presence of our God!
While all around, about us
The brave, unconquered band,
As guardians and landmarks
The giant mountains stand.

Not alone for gold and silver
Is Arizona great.
But with graves of heroes sleeping,
All the land is consecrate!
O, come and live beside us
However far ye roam
Come and help us build up temples
And name those temples "home."

Chorus:
Sing the song that's in your hearts
Sing of the great Southwest,
Thank God, for Arizona
In splendid sunshine dressed.
For thy beauty and thy grandeur,
For thy regal robes so sheen
We hail thee Arizona
Our Goddess and our queen.

"Arizona"
Words and music by Rex Allen Jr.

I love you, Arizona;
Your mountains, deserts and
    streams;
The rise of Dos Cabezas
And the outlaws I see in my
    dreams;

I love you, Arizona,
Superstitions and all;
The warmth you give at sunrise;
Your sunsets put music in us all.

Chorus:
Oo, Arizona;
You're the magic in me;
Oo, Arizona,
You're the life-blood of me;

I love you, Arizona;
Desert dust on the wind;
The sage and cactus are
    blooming,
And the smell of the rain on
    your skin.

(Chorus)

FAMOUS PEOPLE

Apache Kid (ca. 1867–ca. 1910), American Indian outlaw

Babbitt, Bruce (1938–), politician

Carbajal, Michael (1967–), boxer

Chávez, César (1927–1993), labor leader

Cochise (ca. 1812–1874), American Indian leader

Espinoza, Louie (1962–), boxer

Geronimo (1829–1909), American Indian leader

Goldwater, Barry (1909–1998), politician

Jacobs, Helen Hull (1908–1997), tennis player

Kino, Eusebio Francisco (1645–1711), mapmaker and missionary

Luke, Frank, Jr. (1897–1918), fighter pilot

McCain, John (1936–), politician

Mingus, Charles (1922–1979), jazz musician

Nicks, Stevie (1948–), singer and songwriter

O'Connor, Sandra Day (1930–), Supreme Court justice

Poston, Charles (1825–1902), politician known as the Father of Arizona

Ronstadt, Linda (1946–), singer

Spade, David (1964–), comedian and actor

Strug, Kerri (1977–), gymnast and Olympic medalist

Udall, Stewart (1920–), politician

TO FIND OUT MORE

At the Library

Bierhorst, John, and Wendy Watson (illustrator). *Is My Friend at Home?: Pueblo Fireside Tales.* New York: Farrar Straus Giroux, 2001.

Gowan, Barbara, and Katherine Larson (illustrator). *G Is for Grand Canyon: An Arizona Alphabet.* Chelsea, Mich.: Sleeping Bear Press, 2002.

Hill, Mary. *Sandra Day O'Connor.* New York: Children's Press, 2003.

Krull, Kathleen, and Yuyi Morales (illustrator). *Harvesting Hope: The Story of Cesar Chavez.* San Diego: Harcourt, Inc., 2003.

Weintraub, Aileen. *The Grand Canyon: The Widest Canyon.* New York: PowerKids Press, 2001.

On the Web

Visit our home page for lots of links about Arizona: *http://www.childsworld.com/links*

Note to Parents, Teachers, and Librarians: We routinely verify our Web links to make sure they are safe, active sites—so encourage your readers to check them out!

Places to Visit or Contact

Arizona Historical Society
949 East Second Street
Tucson, AZ 85719
502/628-5774
For more information about the history of Arizona

Arizona Office of Tourism
1110 West Washington, Suite 155
Phoenix, AZ 85007
866/275-5816
For more information about traveling in Arizona

INDEX

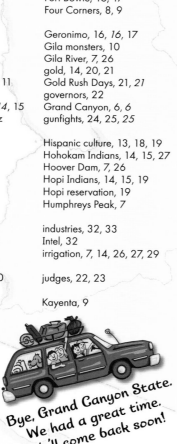

Bye, Grand Canyon State. We had a great time. We'll come back soon!

JUL 1 0 2007

27¹⁰   18(8)

DISCARD